Family Heritage Journal

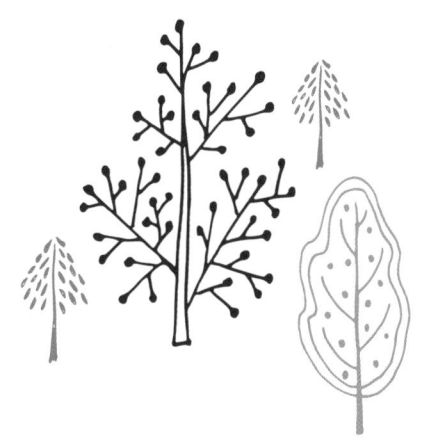

Family Heritage Journal

HISTORY, STORIES, AND CHERISHED KEEPSAKES

Anna Katz

Bluestreak
BOOKS

Bluestreak Books is an imprint of Weldon Owen,
a Bonnier Publishing USA company
www.bonnierpublishingusa.com

Edited and designed by Girl Friday Productions
www.girlfridayproductions.com

Written by Anna Katz

Library of Congress Cataloging in Publication data is available.

ISBN: 978-168188-418-9

First Printed in 2018
10 9 8 7 6 5 4 3 2 1
2018 2019 2020 2021

Printed and bound in China

Illustration Credits:

©Shutterstock/sanuag: cover, 6, 14, 19, 20, 22, 24, 26, 30, 34, 36, 42, 48, 52, 60, 64, 76, 78, 88, 90, 99, 106, 110, 114, 118, 126, 128; ©Shutterstock/Viktoriya Yakubouskaya: cover, endpapers; ©Shutterstock/worldion: 1–3, 60, 108, 109, 128; ©Shutterstock/eaxx: 5, 7, 9, 13, 15, 21, 25, 54–55, 63, 67, 71, 75, 81, 85, 89, 93, 97, 108, 120–125; ©Shutterstock/Iliveinoctober: 8–9, 104–105; ©Shutterstock/vavavka: 12–13, 62–63; ©Shutterstock/smilewithjul: 14, 16–17, 19, 42–46, 68–69, 92–93, 126–127; ©Shutterstock/Olga Zakharova: 15, 30, 106, 107; ©Shutterstock/Laeti-m: 18, 30, 31, 110, 111; ©Shutterstock/Ansty: 20–21; ©Shutterstock/feelplus: 22–23; ©Shutterstock/ Liliana Danila: 24; ©Shutterstock/Akifune: 24–25; ©Shutterstock/ONYXprj: 24; ©Shutterstock/ Ruslana_Vasiukova: 26–27; ©Shutterstock/Vector_dream_team: 28–29; ©Shutterstock/Kaliaha Volha: 32–33, 47, 49–53, 56–57, 60–61, 86–89, 99–101, 111, 126; ©Shutterstock/Vector_Hut: 34–35; ©Shutterstock/Romanova Ekaterina: 34, 36–37, 64–67, 78, 83, 85, 90, 106; ©Shutterstock/ MicroOne: 38–39; ©Shutterstock/Chinch: 40–41; ©Shutterstock/Alenka Karabanova: 44–47, 58–59, 70, 79, 80–82, 84, 94–96, 98, 102–103, 112–113, 115–117; ©Shutterstock/MG Drachal: 48–49, 90–91; ©Shutterstock/tn-prints: 72–73; ©Shutterstock/Guz Anna: 74–75, 118–119; ©Shutterstock/nataliiudina: 76–77; ©Shutterstock/Radiocat: 98, 103, 114–116

This book is dedicated to

_____

_____

_____

_____

Contents

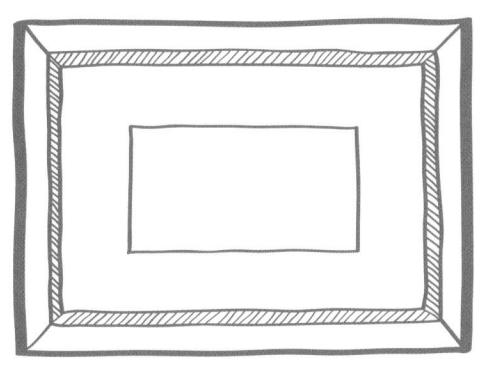

INTRODUCTION

I sustain myself with the love of family.
—Maya Angelou

At its simplest, family is a group of people bonded together—some by blood, some by history, some by friendship and love, and some by choice. These bonds are formed and reformed every day, every year, at every gathering, and they can run many generations deep.

In this journal, you and your family are invited to record and celebrate your heritage—how you came to be family, what makes yours unique, what brings you together, what you believe in.

Some of us know exactly where and when our great-great-great-granddad met our great-great-great-grandmama, or the long history behind the family crest, or the details of the family homestead going back five hundred years. Some of us know little or nothing about our family's past, our origin stories that have been lost to history, the names and homelands of ancestors forgotten in the tumult of war or capture or diaspora, immigration or wanderlust, calamity or the pursuit of happiness. Or simply, of time's passing.

Use this journal to record information about the lives and personalities of loved ones past and present, your family's customs and lineage, and hopes and advice for future generations. You can fill every page out yourself, or share the book with your family members to help complete it.

Throughout the book, you'll see photo frames. In these places, add your own photos or ephemera using your own photo corners or other photo-safe scrapbooking supplies. If you don't have a photo, use the space to write a vivid description of a person or event. There's also an envelope at the back of the book— tuck in keepsakes and memorabilia, which your family can discover and rediscover.

Whatever *you* consider to be family *is* family. Honor yours here.

OUR FAMILY TREE

Some families fit neatly into the shape of a family tree; many do not. In the space here, draw a diagram to fit your family, with lines connecting family members to one another. On these lines, write the nature of the relationship between people (e.g., parent/daughter, brother/sister, spouse, cousin), and include each person's name and date of birth.

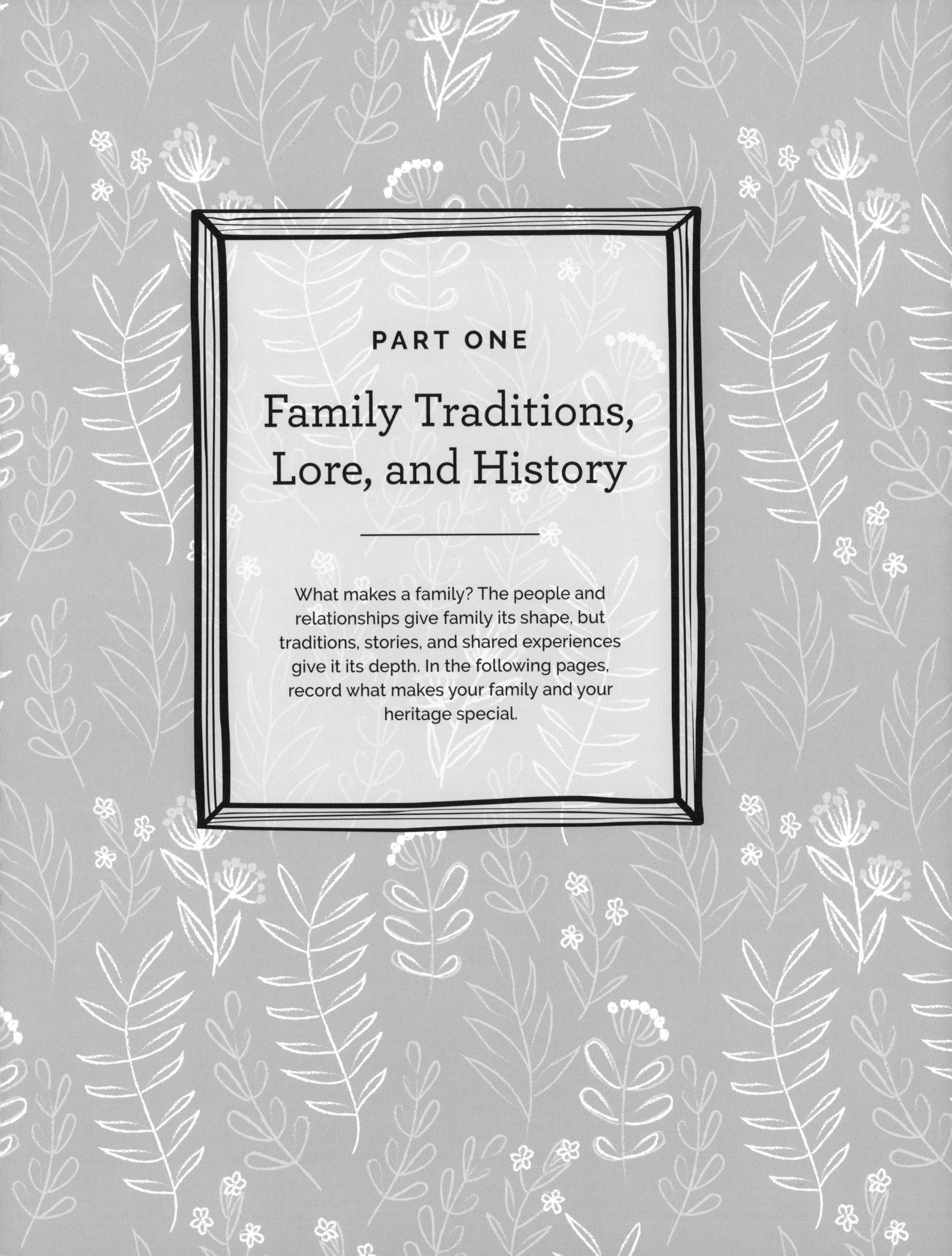

PART ONE

Family Traditions, Lore, and History

———————————

What makes a family? The people and relationships give family its shape, but traditions, stories, and shared experiences give it its depth. In the following pages, record what makes your family and your heritage special.

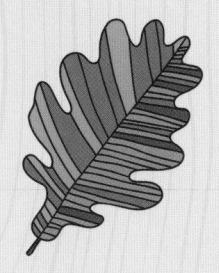

OUR TRADITIONS

It takes an endless amount of history
to make even a little tradition.
—Henry James

Family traditions are beliefs and actions that we do day after day, year after year. They can be linked to religious or cultural beliefs, or they can be everyday rituals that we share.

These are some of the daily, weekly, or yearly traditions our family takes part in:

_____

_____

_____

We celebrate births by: _____

_____

We reunite as a family for: _____

_____

We mourn death and memorialize family members who have passed by: _____

_____

_____

Our traditions around coming of age are: _____

_____

_____

_____

Our traditions around marriage or union are: _____

_____

_____

_____

Write down a story or add a photo from a memorable family tradition. _____

_____

_____

_____

_____

_____

_____

_____

An important holiday or occasion in our family is: _____

_____

_____

We celebrate this holiday or occasion by: _____

_____

_____

_____

_____

_____

_____

An important holiday or occasion in our family is: _____

_____

_____

We celebrate this holiday or occasion by: _____

_____

_____

_____

_____

_____

_____

An important holiday or occasion in our family is: _____

_____

_____

We celebrate this holiday or occasion by: _____

_____

_____

_____

_____

_____

_____

Write down a story from a memorable family gathering. _____

_____

_____

_____

_____

_____

_____

_____

_____

_____

Our cultural or religious beliefs are:

_____

_____

_____

_____

_____

Important texts, ceremonial objects, and symbols of our cultural or religious beliefs are:

_____

_____

_____

_____

_____

Religious or cultural organizations to which our family belongs or has belonged are:

_____

_____

_____

_____

_____

OUR BACKGROUND

Our family's ethnic background is: _____

_____

_____

Languages our family speaks or has spoken are: _____

_____

_____

Write down a favorite traditional prayer, poem, song, or phrase. _____

_____

_____

_____

_____

_____

_____

_____

OUR FAMILY IN THE WORLD

Home is where the heart is.

—Origin unknown

These are places that our family has called home: _____

_____

_____

_____

_____

These places are important to our family's story: _____

_____

_____

_____

_____

These places were hosts to our most memorable celebrations and events: _____

_____

_____

_____

_____

Add a photo or write a story about a family home. _____

IMPORTANT FAMILY JOURNEYS

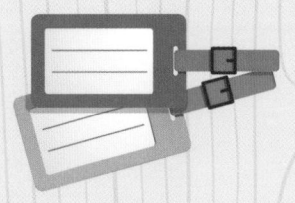

Places our ancestors lived in or came from are: _____

_____

_____

_____

Our ancestors left there because: _____

_____

_____

_____

Places where our ancestors made their new home, and why: _____

_____

_____

_____

_____

Write down places of importance to your family's heritage and history, and fill in those places on the map.

_____

_____

_____

_____

_____

_____

_____

MAP KEY

★ Where we live now

• Places important to my family

---- Journeys

— Moves and immigration

OUR FOOD

After a good dinner one can forgive anybody,
even one's own relations.

—Oscar Wilde

Traditional meals in our family include: _____

_____

_____

A special meal in our family is: _____

_____

_____

Special restaurants where we've had memorable meals together as a family are: _____

_____

_____

The chefs in our family are: _____

_____

_____

Our favorite foods are: _____

_____

_____

Add a photo or write down a story from a memorable family meal. _____

OUR RECIPES

A main-course recipe we have every holiday: _____

_____

_____ makes this recipe.

The history of this recipe is: _____

_____

_____

Ingredients: _____

_____

_____

_____

Instructions: _____

_____

_____

_____

A recipe with specific cultural or religious significance: _____

_____

_____ makes this recipe.

The history of this recipe is: _____

_____

_____

Ingredients: _____

_____

_____

_____

Instructions: _____

_____

_____

_____

_____

_____

_____

_____

_____

_____

_____

A recipe shared among generations: _____

_____ makes this recipe.

The history of this recipe is: _____

_____

_____

Ingredients: _____

_____

_____

Instructions: _____

_____

_____

_____

_____

_____

_____

_____

_____

_____

_____

_____

A new recipe we tried and liked: _____

_____

_____ makes this recipe.

The history of this recipe is: _____

_____

_____

Ingredients: _____

_____

_____

_____

Instructions: _____

_____

_____

_____

_____

_____

_____

_____

_____

_____

_____

_____

STORIES, RUMORS, AND TALL TALES

A legend is a story passed down through generations, sometimes expanding through the years. For some families, these stories encapsulate who they are and where they come from. What are some of your family legends?

_____

_____

_____

_____

_____

_____

_____

_____

_____

Our family's best storytellers are: _____

_____

_____

One of their stories goes like this: _____

_____

_____

_____

_____

_____

_____

_____

_____

Another story goes like this: _____

_____

_____

_____

_____

_____

_____

Write down a funny story about your family that is told and retold.

Sad events, though heartbreaking, help shape who we are. Write down a family story about heartbreak or loss, and what it meant for your family.

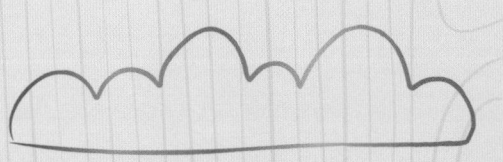

FATEFUL FAMILY EVENTS

A sliding-door event is something that changed the course of your family's history. It can be a death or a birth, a misadventure or a miscommunication, luck or tragedy—any event that would have changed everything if it had or hadn't happened.

A sliding-door event was: _____

_____

This event was momentous or decisive because: _____

_____

_____

_____

_____

_____

_____

_____

A sliding-door event was: _____

_____

This event was momentous or decisive because: _____

_____

_____

_____

_____

_____

_____

_____

_____

_____

A sliding-door event was: _____

_____

This event was momentous or decisive because: _____

_____

_____

_____

_____

_____

_____

OUR FAMILY IN HISTORY

What is history? An echo of the past in the future;
a reflex from the future on the past.
—Victor Hugo

Throughout its generations, our family has witnessed and taken part in history. Whether it's watching a moon walk on TV or voting in a historic election, we were there.

An inspiring or hopeful historic event that our family has witnessed: _____

_____

Year: _____

How various members of our family recall this experience: _____

_____

_____

_____

_____

_____

_____

An inspiring or hopeful historical event that our family has witnessed: _____

Year: _____

How various members of our family recall this experience: _____

_____

_____

_____

_____

_____

_____

An inspiring or hopeful historic event that our family has witnessed: _____

Year: _____

How various members of our family recall this experience: _____

_____

_____

_____

_____

_____

OF COURSE, HISTORY INCLUDES TIMES OF TURMOIL, TOO. WE OR OUR FAMILY MEMBERS REMEMBER THESE DIFFICULT OR TUMULTUOUS EVENTS.

A difficult or tumultuous historic event our family has witnessed: _____

_____

Year: _____

How we endured or took part: _____

_____

_____

_____

_____

A difficult or tumultuous historic event our family has witnessed: _____

_____

Year: _____

How we endured or took part: _____

_____

_____

_____

_____

_____

A difficult or tumultuous historic event our family has witnessed: _____

_____

Year: _____

How we endured or took part: _____

_____

_____

_____

_____

_____

_____

_____

A difficult or tumultuous historic event our family has witnessed: _____

_____

Year: _____

How we endured or took part: _____

_____

_____

_____

_____

_____

TECHNOLOGY ADVANCES DRIVE HISTORY AND ARE THE RESULT OF HISTORY. HERE'S HOW TECHNOLOGY AFFECTED OUR FAMILY.

The first member of our family to own a television was: _____

_____

The first member of our family to fly in an airplane was: _____

_____

The first family member to own a desktop computer was: _____

_____

The first member of our family to write an email was: _____

_____

The first member of our family to use social media was: _____

_____

The first member of our family to own a smartphone was: _____

_____

The oldest member of our family to own a smartphone is: _____

_____

The youngest member of our family to have used a rotary phone is: _____

_____

Other technology worth mentioning is: _____

_____

_____

_____

SOCIAL CHANGE HAPPENS WHEN THE WAY A CULTURE THINKS, FEELS, OR ACTS ABOUT SOMETHING SHIFTS. THIS COULD BE THE MANDATE OF A NEW LAW OR THE DISMANTLING OF AN OLD ONE, ACCEPTANCE OF A LIFESTYLE THAT WAS PREVIOUSLY FROWNED UPON, OR A NEW WAY OF THINKING ABOUT AN IDEOLOGY PREVIOUSLY TAKEN FOR GRANTED.

A big social change our family or family members have witnessed or taken part in was:

_____

_____

Before that, the world was: _____

_____

_____

_____

A big social change our family or family members have witnessed or taken part in was:

_____

_____

Before that, the world was: _____

_____

_____

_____

OUR FAMILY IN THE NEWS

Has a family member been honorably mentioned? Had fifteen minutes of fame?

Regularly occupied a space above the fold? In the envelope at the back of the book,

archive clippings in which family members were featured.

Family member featured: _____

_____

The story: _____

_____

_____

_____

_____

_____

_____

Family member featured: _____

_____

The story: _____

_____

_____

_____

_____

_____

_____

_____

_____

Family member featured: _____

_____

The story: _____

_____

_____

_____

_____

_____

_____

Family member featured: _____

_____

The story: _____

_____

_____

_____

_____

_____

_____

_____

Family member featured: _____

_____

The story: _____

_____

_____

_____

_____

_____

_____

Family member featured: _____

_____

The story: _____

_____

_____

_____

_____

_____

_____

_____

_____

_____

Family member featured: _____

_____

The story: _____

_____

_____

_____

_____

_____

_____

THESE STORIES DIDN'T MAKE THE HEADLINES—BUT PROBABLY SHOULD HAVE!

Family members who would have been featured: _____

_____

The stories: _____

_____

_____

_____

_____

_____

_____

_____

_____

_____

_____

_____

_____

_____

Family members who would have been featured: _____

_____

The stories: _____

_____

_____

_____

_____

_____

_____

_____

_____

_____

_____

_____

_____

_____

_____

_____

_____

_____

FAMILY SAYINGS, JOKES, AND NICKNAMES

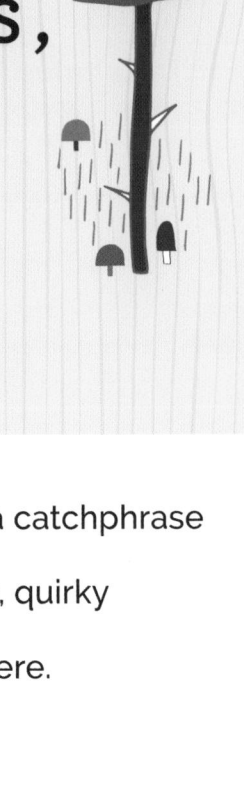

I like good, strong words that mean something.
—Louisa May Alcott

Is there something that you or another family member says all the time, a catchphrase or an expression that you or they are known for? What about inside jokes, quirky phrases, odd maxims, or funny nicknames? Record your family's words here.

Saying: _____

_____

Who said it: _____

_____

Saying: _____

_____

Who said it: _____

_____

Saying: _____

_____

_____

Who said it: _____

_____

_____

Saying: _____

_____

_____

Who said it: _____

_____

_____

Saying: _____

_____

_____

Who said it: _____

_____

_____

Saying: _____

_____

_____

Who said it: _____

_____

JOKES

Family member: _____

Their joke: _____

_____

Family member: _____

Their joke: _____

_____

Family member: _____

Their joke: _____

_____

Family member: _____

Their joke: _____

_____

Family member: _____

Their joke: _____

_____

_____

NICKNAMES AND WORDPLAY

Nickname	Their real name	Who came up with the nickname
--------------------	------------------	----------------------
--------------------	------------------	----------------------
--------------------	------------------	----------------------
--------------------	------------------	----------------------
--------------------	------------------	----------------------
--------------------	------------------	----------------------

Here's the story behind one of those nicknames: _____

_____

_____

_____

Words we use in our family that we don't hear elsewhere: _____

_____

_____

_____

Funny words family members said when they were babies: _____

_____

_____

_____

FAMILY TREASURES

An heirloom is any keepsake, passed down through many generations or recently given to a family member by another. It can be anything that is cherished or evokes a memory—an old letter, a set of china, a handkerchief, a diamond ring. Include keepsakes currently in the family's possession and those that have been lost or left behind.

Heirloom #1: _____

This heirloom was passed down from: _____

The story of this heirloom: _____

_____

_____

_____

What this heirloom means to our family: _____

_____

_____

_____

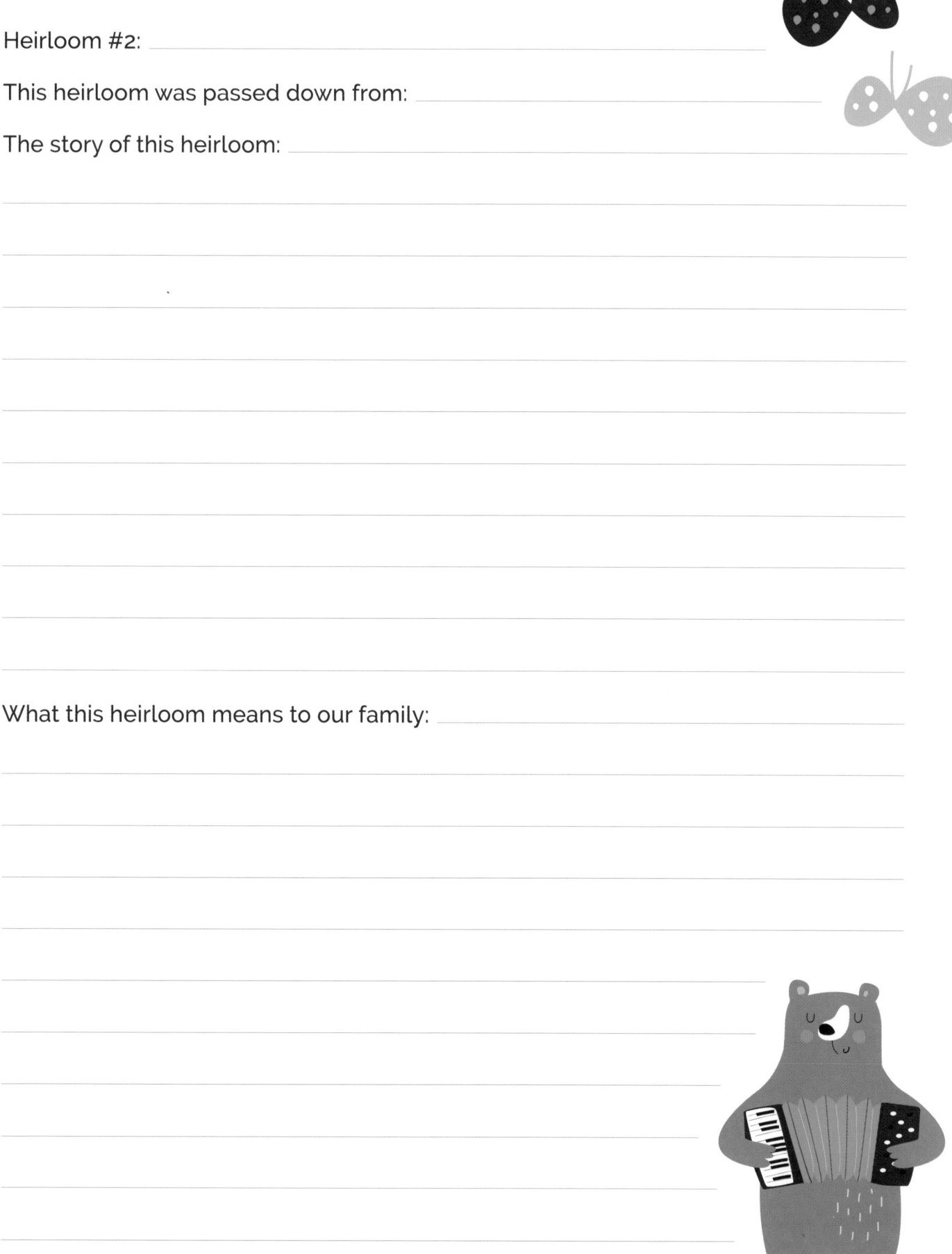

Heirloom #2: _____

This heirloom was passed down from: _____

The story of this heirloom: _____

_____

_____

_____

_____

_____

_____

_____

_____

What this heirloom means to our family: _____

_____

_____

_____

_____

_____

_____

Heirloom #3: _____

This heirloom was passed down from: _____

The story of this heirloom: _____

_____

_____

_____

_____

_____

_____

_____

_____

What this heirloom means to our family: _____

_____

_____

_____

_____

_____

_____

Heirloom #4: _____

This heirloom was passed down from: _____

The story of this heirloom: _____

_____

_____

_____

_____

_____

_____

_____

_____

What this heirloom means to our family: _____

_____

_____

_____

_____

_____

_____

_____

Heirloom #5: _____

This heirloom was passed down from: _____

The story of this heirloom: _____

_____

_____

_____

_____

_____

_____

_____

What this heirloom means to our family: _____

_____

_____

_____

_____

_____

_____

Heirloom #6: _____

This heirloom was passed down from: _____

The story of this heirloom: _____

_____

_____

_____

_____

_____

_____

_____

_____

_____

What this heirloom means to our family: _____

_____

_____

_____

_____

_____

_____

_____

Heirloom #7: _____

This heirloom was passed down from: _____

The story of this heirloom: _____

_____

_____

_____

_____

_____

_____

_____

_____

What this heirloom means to our family: _____

_____

_____

_____

_____

_____

_____

Heirloom #8: _____

This heirloom was passed down from: _____

The story of this heirloom: _____

_____

_____

_____

_____

_____

_____

_____

_____

_____

What this heirloom means to our family: _____

_____

_____

_____

_____

_____

_____

_____

FAMILY VALUES

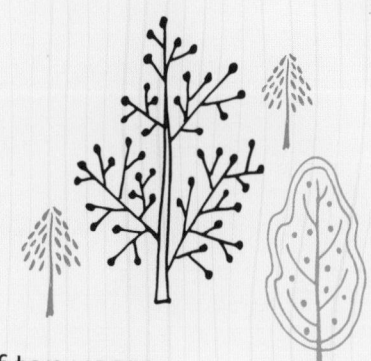

If you think in terms of a year, plant a seed; if in terms of ten years,
plant trees; if in terms of one hundred years, teach the people.
—Confucius

Our family's most cherished values are: _____

_____

_____

_____

_____

_____

_____

_____

_____

_____

_____

_____

_____

We do our best to uphold these values by expressing them in the following ways:

PART TWO

Our Family Members

Every family is as unique as each of its members. In the following pages, record details and descriptions of the great-grandparents, grandparents, aunts and uncles, parents, children, nieces and nephews, close friends, and even pets who comprise your family tree. The prompts in this section will help you record what's unique about your family.

ABOUT MY GENERATION

Families are made up of generations. These are the siblings, cousins, and close family friends who occupy the similar branches of the family tree.

For each member of the generation, fill in the prompts. The description can be whatever you want to include: details about personality, vocation, education, most vivid memory, passions, and more. Start with yourself and then fill in information for others, or pass this journal among family members to complete for themselves.

> THE PEOPLE IN MY GENERATION
>
> WERE BORN BETWEEN THE YEARS
>
> _____ AND _____.

MEMBERS OF THIS GENERATION INCLUDE . . .

Name: _____

Date of birth: _____

Place of birth: _____

Parents: _____

Relationship: _____

Spouse: _____

Children: _____

Description: _____

_____

_____

_____

Name: _____

Date of birth: _____

Place of birth: _____

Parents: _____

Relationship: _____

Spouse: _____

Children: _____

Description: _____

_____

_____

MEMBERS OF THIS GENERATION INCLUDE . . .

Name: _____

Date of birth: _____

Place of birth: _____

Parents: _____

Relationship: _____

Spouse: _____

Children: _____

Description: _____

_____

_____

_____

_____

Name: _____

Date of birth: _____

Place of birth: _____

Parents: _____

Relationship: _____

Spouse: _____

Children: _____

Description: _____

_____

_____

_____

Insert a photo of or write a description about a favorite family memory featuring the people in this generation.

MEMBERS OF THIS GENERATION INCLUDE . . .

Name: _____

Date of birth: _____

Place of birth: _____

Parents: _____

Relationship: _____

Spouse: _____

Children: _____

Description: _____

_____

_____

_____

Name: _____

Date of birth: _____

Place of birth: _____

Parents: _____

Relationship: _____

Spouse: _____

Children: _____

Description: _____

_____

_____

MEMBERS OF THIS GENERATION INCLUDE . . .

Name: _____

Date of birth: _____

Place of birth: _____

Parents: _____

Relationship: _____

Spouse: _____

Children: _____

Description: _____

_____

_____

_____

_____

Name: _____

Date of birth: _____

Place of birth: _____

Parents: _____

Relationship: _____

Spouse: _____

Children: _____

Description: _____

_____

_____

_____

MEMBERS OF THIS GENERATION INCLUDE . . .

Name: _____

Date of birth: _____

Place of birth: _____

Parents: _____

Relationship: _____

Spouse: _____

Children: _____

Description: _____

_____

_____

_____

Name: _____

Date of birth: _____

Place of birth: _____

Parents: _____

Relationship: _____

Spouse: _____

Children: _____

Description: _____

_____

_____

_____

THIS GENERATION IN HISTORY

- What technological advancements happened during these years?

- What was going on in pop culture during this time?

- What were some significant social and political events during this time?

Write down a funny story that involved you and your siblings, cousins, or close
friends—one that you retell during family gatherings and that always makes you laugh.

_____

_____

_____

_____

_____

_____

_____

_____

_____

_____

_____

_____

_____

_____

MEMBERS OF THIS GENERATION INCLUDE . . .

Name: _____

Date of birth: _____

Place of birth: _____

Parents: _____

Relationship: _____

Spouse: _____

Children: _____

Description: _____

_____

_____

_____

Name: _____

Date of birth: _____

Place of birth: _____

Parents: _____

Relationship: _____

Spouse: _____

Children: _____

Description: _____

_____

_____

MEMBERS OF THIS GENERATION INCLUDE . . .

Name: _____

Date of birth: _____

Place of birth: _____

Parents: _____

Relationship: _____

Spouse: _____

Children: _____

Description: _____

_____

_____

_____

Name: _____

Date of birth: _____

Place of birth: _____

Parents: _____

Relationship: _____

Spouse: _____

Children: _____

Description: _____

_____

_____

Insert a photo of or write a description about a favorite family memory featuring the people in this generation.

_____

_____

_____

_____

_____

_____

_____

_____

_____

_____

_____

_____

_____

_____

MEMORABLE FAMILY PETS

Pets are also part of the family! Here are some of our favorite furry family members.

Name: _____

Date of birth: _____

Whose pet: _____

Where we got this pet: _____

Description: _____

_____

Name: _____

Date of birth: _____

Whose pet: _____

Where we got this pet: _____

Description: _____

_____

Name: _____

Date of birth: _____

Whose pet: _____

Where we got this pet: _____

Description: _____

_____

_____

_____

Name: _____

Date of birth: _____

Whose pet: _____

Where we got this pet: _____

Description: _____

_____

_____

_____

Name: _____

Date of birth: _____

Whose pet: _____

Where we got this pet: _____

Description: _____

_____

 _____

ABOUT OUR OLDER GENERATIONS

This generation is made up of those who came before: the grandparents, great-grandparents, great-great-grandparents, and so on.

For each member of the generation, fill in the prompts. In the description, write what you or others in the family remember about this person: details about their personality, vocation, education, passions, your most vivid memory of them. You can fill in what you remember, and interview other family members about their memories or pass this journal among them to complete the prompts.

Describe if and how members of the current generations may have revealed similar traits in their personalities.

THE PEOPLE IN THESE GENERATIONS
WERE BORN BEFORE

- - - - - - - - - - - - - - .

MEMBERS OF THE OLDER GENERATIONS INCLUDE . . .

Name: _____

Date of birth: _____

Place of birth: _____

Parents: _____

Relationship: _____

Spouse: _____

Children: _____

Description: _____

_____

_____

_____

Name: _____

Date of birth: _____

Place of birth: _____

Parents: _____

Relationship: _____

Spouse: _____

Children: _____

Description: _____

_____

_____

MEMBERS OF THE OLDER GENERATIONS INCLUDE . . .

Name: _____

Date of birth: _____

Place of birth: _____

Parents: _____

Relationship: _____

Spouse: _____

Children: _____

Description: _____

_____

_____

_____

Name: _____

Date of birth: _____

Place of birth: _____

Parents: _____

Relationship: _____

Spouse: _____

Children: _____

Description: _____

_____

_____

Insert a photo of or write a description about a favorite family memory featuring the people in this generation.

MEMBERS OF THE OLDER GENERATIONS INCLUDE . . .

Name: _____

Date of birth: _____

Place of birth: _____

Parents: _____

Relationship: _____

Spouse: _____

Children: _____

Description: _____

_____

_____

_____

Name: _____

Date of birth: _____

Place of birth: _____

Parents: _____

Relationship: _____

Spouse: _____

Children: _____

Description: _____

_____

_____

_____

MEMBERS OF THE OLDER GENERATIONS INCLUDE . . .

Name: _____

Date of birth: _____

Place of birth: _____

Parents: _____

Relationship: _____

Spouse: _____

Children: _____

Description: _____

_____

_____

_____

_____

Name: _____

Date of birth: _____

Place of birth: _____

Parents: _____

Relationship: _____

Spouse: _____

Children: _____

Description: _____

_____

_____

MEMBERS OF THE OLDER GENERATIONS INCLUDE . . .

Name: _____

Date of birth: _____

Place of birth: _____

Parents: _____

Relationship: _____

Spouse: _____

Children: _____

Description: _____

_____

_____

_____

Name: _____

Date of birth: _____

Place of birth: _____

Parents: _____

Relationship: _____

Spouse: _____

Children: _____

Description: _____

_____

_____

THIS GENERATION IN HISTORY

- What was the style of dress for older generations?

- What were some big technological advancements that impacted older generations?

- What were some significant social and political events that occurred?

MEMBERS OF THE OLDER GENERATIONS INCLUDE . . .

Name: _____

Date of birth: _____

Place of birth: _____

Parents: _____

Relationship: _____

Spouse: _____

Children: _____

Description: _____

_____

_____

_____

Name: _____

Date of birth: _____

Place of birth: _____

Parents: _____

Relationship: _____

Spouse: _____

Children: _____

Description: _____

_____

_____

Write a description of a family legend that took place during an older generation.

OLDER GENERATIONS' PETS

Pets are also part of the family! These are the pets of older relatives whom you remember playing with as a child, or whose stories you grew up hearing.

Pets of the past: _____

_____

_____

_____

_____

_____

_____

_____

_____

_____

Add a photo or continue writing descriptions of animals from your family's past.

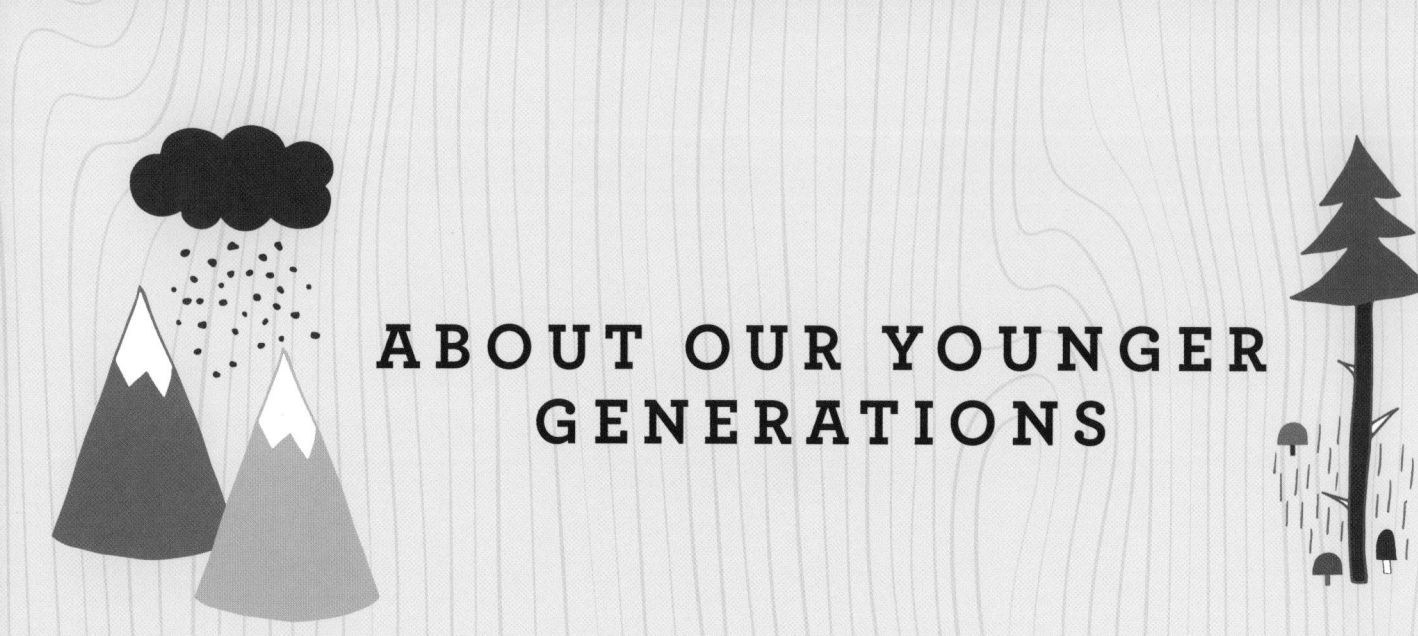

ABOUT OUR YOUNGER GENERATIONS

This generation is made up of those who occupy the newest branches of the family tree: the young siblings, cousins, and family friends.

For each member of the generation, write the name, date of birth, place of birth, and relationship to others in the generation. The description can be whatever you want to include: details about personality, vocation, education, most vivid memory, passions, etc. You can fill in for yourself, get an older person to help you, and pass this journal among family members to complete for themselves.

> ## THE PEOPLE IN THIS GENERATION WERE BORN AFTER
>
> - - - - - - - - - - - - - - - .

MEMBERS OF THE YOUNGER GENERATIONS INCLUDE . . .

Name: _____

Date of birth: _____

Place of birth: _____

Parents: _____

Relationship: _____

Spouse: _____

Children: _____

Description: _____

_____

_____

_____

_____

Name: _____

Date of birth: _____

Place of birth: _____

Parents: _____

Relationship: _____

Spouse: _____

Children: _____

Description: _____

_____

_____

MEMBERS OF THE YOUNGER GENERATIONS INCLUDE . . .

Name: _____

Date of birth: _____

Place of birth: _____

Parents: _____

Relationship: _____

Spouse: _____

Children: _____

Description: _____

_____

_____

_____

Name: _____

Date of birth: _____

Place of birth: _____

Parents: _____

Relationship: _____

Spouse: _____

Children: _____

Description: _____

_____

Insert a photo of or write a description about a favorite family memory featuring the people in this generation.

MEMBERS OF THE YOUNGER GENERATIONS INCLUDE . . .

Name: _____

Date of birth: _____

Place of birth: _____

Parents: _____

Relationship: _____

Spouse: _____

Children: _____

Description: _____

_____

_____

_____

_____

Name: _____

Date of birth: _____

Place of birth: _____

Parents: _____

Relationship: _____

Spouse: _____

Children: _____

Description: _____

_____

_____

MEMBERS OF THE YOUNGER GENERATIONS INCLUDE . . .

Name: _____

Date of birth: _____

Place of birth: _____

Parents: _____

Relationship: _____

Spouse: _____

Children: _____

Description: _____

_____

_____

_____

Name: _____

Date of birth: _____

Place of birth: _____

Parents: _____

Relationship: _____

Spouse: _____

Children: _____

Description: _____

_____

_____

MEMBERS OF THE YOUNGER GENERATIONS INCLUDE . . .

Name: _____

Date of birth: _____

Place of birth: _____

Parents: _____

Relationship: _____

Spouse: _____

Children: _____

Description: _____

_____

_____

_____

Name: _____

Date of birth: _____

Place of birth: _____

Parents: _____

Relationship: _____

Spouse: _____

Children: _____

Description: _____

_____

_____

THE YOUNGER GENERATION IN HISTORY

- What technological advancements are happening?

- What's going on in pop culture?

- What are some significant current social and political events?

MEMBERS OF THE YOUNGER GENERATIONS INCLUDE . . .

Name: _____

Date of birth: _____

Place of birth: _____

Parents: _____

Relationship: _____

Spouse: _____

Children: _____

Description: _____

_____

_____

_____

Name: _____

Date of birth: _____

Place of birth: _____

Parents: _____

Relationship: _____

Spouse: _____

Children: _____

Description: _____

_____

_____

THE YOUNGER GENERATIONS' PETS

WHO ARE THE PERFECT PETS THAT YOUNGER GENERATIONS LOVE?

Name: _____

Date of birth: _____

Whose pet: _____

Where we got this pet: _____

Description: _____

_____

Name: _____

Date of birth: _____

Where we got this pet: _____

Whose pet: _____

Description: _____

_____

Name: _____

Date of birth: _____

Whose pet: _____

Where we got this pet: _____

Description: _____

_____

_____

_____

Name: _____

Date of birth: _____

Whose pet: _____

Where we got this pet: _____

Description: _____

_____

_____

_____

Name: _____

Date of birth: _____

Where we got this pet: _____

Whose pet: _____

Description: _____

_____

_____

_____

Interview members of the younger generation, or ask them to write down lessons that they have learned from your family's past. Whether it's learning how to make the family apple pie recipe just right, learning a family baptism ritual, or understanding the value of perseverance from your family legends, it's wonderful to see ideas spread across generations.

Write down some dreams that members of this generation have for the future.

Write down a story about members of the younger generations interacting with members of older generations. What magic or mishap may have occurred?

ABOUT FAMILY FRIENDS AND NEIGHBORS

Friends are the siblings God never gave us.

—Mencius

Not all family are blood relatives. Write about friends or neighbors who have come to feel like family.

Name: _____

Date of birth: _____

Place of birth: _____

Spouse: _____

Children: _____

We know this person because: _____

_____

This person is like family because: _____

_____

Description: _____

_____

_____

_____

Name: _____

Date of birth: _____

Place of birth: _____

Spouse: _____

Children: _____

We know this person because: _____

_____

This person is like family because: _____

_____

Description: _____

_____

_____

Name: _____

Date of birth: _____

Place of birth: _____

Spouse: _____

Children: _____

We know this person because: _____

_____

This person is like family because: _____

_____

Description: _____

_____

_____

Add a photo or write down a memory involving a friend who feels like family. _____

_____

_____

_____

_____

_____

_____

_____

_____

_____

_____

_____

Name: _____

Date of birth: _____

Place of birth: _____

Spouse: _____

Children: _____

We know this person because: _____

_____

This person is like family because: _____

_____

Description: _____

_____

_____

Name: _____

Date of birth: _____

Place of birth: _____

Spouse: _____

Children: _____

We know this person because: _____

_____

This person is like family because: _____

_____

Description: _____

_____

THIS FAMILY LOVES . . .

Call or text your family members, and find out some of their favorite things.

FAMILY MEMBERS' FAVORITE BOOKS

Name   Book

--------------------------------   --

--------------------------------   --

--------------------------------   --

--------------------------------   --

FAMILY MEMBERS' FAVORITE TV SHOWS

Name   Show

--------------------------------   --

--------------------------------   --

--------------------------------   --

--------------------------------   --

FAMILY MEMBERS' FAVORITE MOVIES

Name   Movie

------------------------------   ------------------------------------

------------------------------   ------------------------------------

------------------------------   ------------------------------------

------------------------------   ------------------------------------

------------------------------   ------------------------------------

FAMILY MEMBERS' FAVORITE BANDS

Name   Band

------------------------------   ------------------------------------

------------------------------   ------------------------------------

------------------------------   ------------------------------------

------------------------------   ------------------------------------

------------------------------   ------------------------------------

FAMILY MEMBERS' FAVORITE SONGS

Name   Song

------------------------------   ------------------------------------

------------------------------   ------------------------------------

------------------------------   ------------------------------------

------------------------------   ------------------------------------

FAMILY MEMBERS' BEST SUBJECTS IN SCHOOL

Name   Subject

----------------------------------   --

----------------------------------   --

----------------------------------   --

----------------------------------   --

----------------------------------   --

FAMILY MEMBERS' FAVORITE FOODS

Name   Food

----------------------------------   --

----------------------------------   --

----------------------------------   --

----------------------------------   --

----------------------------------   --

FAMILY MEMBERS' FAVORITE BOARD OR CARD GAMES

Name   Game

----------------------------------   --

----------------------------------   --

----------------------------------   --

----------------------------------   --

----------------------------------   --

FAMILY MEMBERS' FAVORITE SPORTS TEAMS

Name   Team

------------------------------------   --

------------------------------------   --

------------------------------------   --

------------------------------------   --

------------------------------------   --

FAMILY MEMBERS' FAVORITE CARS

Name   Car

------------------------------------   --

------------------------------------   --

------------------------------------   --

------------------------------------   --

------------------------------------   --

FAMILY MEMBERS' FAVORITE VACATION SPOTS

Name   Vacation spot

------------------------------------   --

------------------------------------   --

------------------------------------   --

------------------------------------   --

------------------------------------   --

HOPE AND ADVICE FOR THE NEXT GENERATIONS

Hope is the pillar that holds up the world.

—Pliny the Elder

As younger generations grow older and your family expands into the future, they will look to their heritage for grounding and for direction.

Write down life lessons you've learned, and your hopes and advice for future generations. Interview other family members or share this book with them to add their thoughts and hopes as well.

Name: _____

Valuable life lessons I learned from other family members: _____

_____

_____

My hopes for future generations: _____

_____

_____

My advice for future generations: _____

_____

Name: _____

Valuable life lessons I learned from other family members: _____

_____

_____

My hopes for future generations: _____

_____

_____

My advice for future generations: _____

_____

_____

_____

_____

Name: _____

Valuable life lessons I learned from other family members: _____

_____

_____

My hopes for future generations: _____

_____

_____

My advice for future generations: _____

_____

_____

_____

Name: _____

Valuable life lessons I learned from other family members: _____

_____

_____

My hopes for future generations: _____

_____

_____

My advice for future generations: _____

_____

_____

_____

Name: _____

Valuable life lessons I learned from other family members: _____

_____

_____

My hopes for future generations: _____

_____

_____

My advice for future generations: _____

_____

Name: _____

Valuable life lessons I learned from other family members: _____

_____

_____

My hopes for future generations: _____

_____

_____

My advice for future generations: _____

_____

_____

_____

_____

Name: _____

Valuable life lessons I learned from other family members: _____

_____

_____

My hopes for future generations: _____

_____

_____

My advice for future generations: _____

_____

_____

_____

MORE ABOUT OUR FAMILY

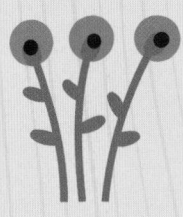

Do you have more family member profiles to add? Need more space to write down great family stories? Use these pages to record whatever you wish.

Add a photo or write down a memory of whatever you wish.

Add a photo or write down a memory of whatever you wish.

Add a photo or write down a memory of whatever you wish. _____

WHAT FAMILY MEANS TO ME

The family is one of nature's masterpieces.
—George Santayana

As you completed the *Family Heritage Journal*, you explored your family's legends and roots, hardships and successes, proudest moments and hilarious times. You thought about people and relationships, both current and in the past. All of these elements and people, actions and reactions, together form the masterpiece of your family—and you.

Write down some closing thoughts about what you learned from the experience of recording your family's details, and what it means to you.

_____

_____

_____

_____

_____

_____

RESOURCES

for Researching and
Recording Your Family Heritage

National Archives

www.archives.gov/research/genealogy/start-research
Access census, military, immigration, naturalization, and land records to find out more about your family members. The website also has Online Learning Resources with videos from genealogy workshops and sections dedicated to African American, Native American, and Asian American heritage.

State Archives

www.archives.gov/research/alic/reference/state-archives
Contact your state archives to determine what historical information is available. Often, you can find state census information as well as Native American and pioneer records.

U.S. Census Burau

www.census.gov/history/www/genealogy
Once necessary forms are completed, census records from 1950 to 2010 can be released by the person named in the records or their legal heir.

The Statue of Liberty—Ellis Island Foundation

www.libertyellisfoundation.org
Search through their database of more than 51 million passenger records.

Genealogy Sites

Subscription services like Ancestry.com and Footnote.com can connect what you know about your genealogy with other registered uses' info, making connections and filling in gaps.

DNA Testing

Different companies focus on different uses for information about your DNA, so research thoroughly before using one. Most companies will send you a kit through the mail to help you gather your DNA, then they'll send the results to you.

Family Interviews

Nothing can substitute for talking to your family and asking questions. Resources like the *Family Heritage Journal* are a great start. Many sites out there offer advice on what questions to ask to trace your roots. Just search the internet for "family genealogy interview."